Science Around Us

Energy

Sally Hewitt

Chrysalis Education

Distributed in the United States by
Smart Apple Media
1980 Lookout Drive
North Mankato, MN 56003

Copyright © Chrysalis Books PLC 2003

ISBN 1-93198-393-3

The Library of Congress control number 2003102403

Editorial manager: Joyce Bentley
Project editor: Clare Weaver
Designer: Wladek Szechter
Picture researcher: Aline Morley
Consultant: Helen Walters

Printed in Hong Kong

10 9 8 7 6 5 4 3 2 1

Words in **bold** can be found in Words to remember on page 30.

Picture credits
cover ; main picture ; Royalty Free/Corbis
Inset (L-R) Angela Hampton/Bubbles, Roger Ressmeyer/Corbis, Owaki – Kulla/Corbis, Novosti Press Agency/SPL; Back Cover ; Maximilian Stock/SPL © Bubbles P5 Pauline Cutler, P8 Jennie Woodcock, P9 Loisjoy Thurston, P15 Susanna Price, P21 Angela Hampton, P23 Jennie Woodcock, P24 Loisjoy Thurston, P25 Loisjoy Thurston © Corbis P4 (L) Guy Motil , P6 Photowood Inc, P7 Roy McMahon, P10 Ariel Skelley, P11 Norbert Schaefer, P16 Jim Cummins,P19 Roger Ressmeyer, P22 Lester Lefkowitz, P26 Owaki - Kulla, P27(R) Royalty-Free © Getty P4 (R) Ross Whitaker, P12 Chris Warbey, P27 John K. Humble, P14 Stephen Simpson © SPL P1 Maximilian Stock Ltd, P13 Anthony Mercieca, P17 Hugh Turvey, P18 Tek Image,

Contents

What is energy?

Energy makes things happen. Animals and plants can live, grow, and move—and **machines** are able to **work** hard—because of energy.

Electricity gives the dishwasher the energy it needs to work.

The Sun is a giant ball of burning gas that gives Earth heat and light. Energy on our planet Earth starts with the Sun.

Heat, light, sound, movement, and **electricity** are all different kinds of energy.

When you run out of energy, you start to feel hungry and tired—and you need to have something to eat.

We get our energy from the food we eat. This energy is stored in our muscles and we use it whenever we move.

plants

Plants don't have to hunt for food. They use energy from sunlight to make their own food from air, water, and goodness in the soil.

An apple tree stores energy from sunlight in its apples. The seeds inside an apple use this energy to grow into a new apple tree.

Fruit is full of the good things a new plant needs to grow. This is why fruit is good food for you to eat.

Plants trap energy from the sun in the green color in their leaves. They use it to make their food.

When you eat a juicy apple, you become full of energy from sunlight, too.

Full of energy

You use energy day and night. How much energy you use depends on how hard you work and how busy you are.

You use up a lot of energy running and jumping because your body is working hard.

The muscles you use for
moving around have a rest while you sleep.

You use less energy
when you are asleep, but
your body is still working.
You keep breathing, your
heart goes on beating,
and your brain keeps
on working.

In your sleep,
your heart
beats less
often and your
breathing
slows down.

Food

All living things and many machines need to burn **fuel** to give them energy. The fuel our bodies burn is called food.

We need to eat regular meals to keep our bodies supplied with fuel.

Food gives us energy and it helps to keep us strong and healthy, too. It is important to choose food that is good for us.

Eating too much of the wrong kind of food is not good for us. Without enough food to eat, we soon become hungry, tired, and weak.

You need to drink plenty of water, as well as eat food for energy.

11

Animals

Lions are meat-eaters. They use up a lot of energy hunting for their food. The meat they eat gives them so much energy, they don't need to hunt every day.

After a good meal, lions rest and sleep. This helps them to save energy.

Some birds save energy
by **gliding** for long distances
without flapping their wings.

Birds that eat grubs and
insects work hard to find enough
food to give them energy
to fly.

Birds use up an enormous amount
of energy when they fly.

Movement and sound

There are different kinds of energy. When something moves it has movement energy.

A bus has movement energy as it drives along the road. You have movement energy as well when you run to catch a bus.

This baby moves when she bangs the drum. This movement energy turns into sound energy and she hears a banging noise.

When you bang a drum you make sound energy. When you bang harder you use more energy and make a louder sound.

Heat and light

When you run around, your body makes heat energy. You start to feel hot and sweaty. The faster and harder you run, the hotter and sweatier you feel.

When you sweat, little drops of water form on your skin. They help to cool you down.

Never touch a glowing light bulb. It gives out enough heat energy to burn you.

We use heat energy to keep warm and cook our food.

A light bulb gives out light and heat energy. The thin wire inside the bulb gets very hot and glows strongly enough to light up a room.

Coal

Coal is a kind of fuel formed from plants that died millions of years ago. A piece of coal is full of energy.

Coal gives out heat and light energy when it burns.

The coal is brought up to the surface.
Coal is burned to give out heat energy.

Coal is found deep
underground, buried
under layers of rock
and soil. Miners dig out
the coal with drills and
big cutting machines.

When we burn
coal, we are using
energy from sunlight.
This energy is stored
in plants from millions
of years ago.

Gas and oil

Gas and **oil** are two more kinds of fuel that we burn to make energy. They are found deep under ground, both on land and at the bottom of the sea.

Long pipes carry oil and gas back to land, from the oil platform out at sea.

When a car has burned up all its gasoline it runs out of energy. We have to fill it up again to keep it moving.

We cook food using the heat energy from burning gas.

Oil is made into a fuel called **gasoline** in an oil refinery. A car engine burns gas to give it the energy to move.

Electricity

Electricity is another form of energy. **Lightning** is a very powerful kind of natural electricity. We can make electricity and use it to power the things we use every day.

Coal, oil, and gas are burned in power stations. This makes heat which is turned into electricity.

Electricity from power stations flows along thick **cables** to supply towns and cities.

When you turn on a switch, electricity flows along the wire and gives the television energy it needs to work.

Electricity comes into our homes through **sockets** in the walls. Lights, heaters, and machines that use electricity have plugs that are fitted into the sockets.

Batteries

A **battery** is a packet of **stored** energy. There are **chemicals** inside it. When a wire is connected to both ends of the battery, the chemicals start to change and make electricity.

A battery gives a personal stereo the energy it needs to work.

Batteries are very useful for powering small things that you need to carry around with you, such as a flashlight.

Machines that use batteries don't need to be plugged into sockets.

When the chemicals inside a battery run out, they won't make any more electricity. You will need a new battery.

Sun, water, and wind

We use so much energy to power machines that, one day, we will burn up all the coal, oil, and gas on Earth.

Solar panels trap energy from the sun to heat up water and make electricity.

Energy from moving water is used to make electricity in a **hydroelectric power** station.

Energy from turning windmills is used to make electricity on a wind farm.

Sun, wind, and water can give us energy that will never run out.

MAKE BUTTERFLIES FLUTTER

Create static electricity and watch it make tissue-paper butterflies move.

YOU WILL NEED:

- colored tissue paper
- paints
- paintbrush
- a sheet of white paper
- scissors
- Ping-Pong ball
- length of thread
- Scotch tape

1 Cut out about six small butterfly shapes from colored tissue paper. (Make each about 2in. across and 1in. high.)

2 Paint three big colorful flowers on the white paper.

3 Tape the length of thread onto the Ping-Pong ball.

4 Put two butterflies on each painted flower.

5 Rub the Ping-Pong ball against a woolen sweater for a few moments to make a kind of electricity called static electricity.

See if you can make the butterflies flutter from flower to flower.

6 Swing the ball over the butterflies. Watch the static electricity from the ball make them flutter.

battery A packet of stored energy used to power machines. Electricity is made when chemicals inside the battery change.

cables Long metal wires, wrapped in plastic, which carry electricity from power stations into our homes. Electricity can flow along the metal, but it cannot flow through plastic.

chemicals What everything is made up of, including our own bodies. The chemicals inside a battery make electricity.

coal A kind of fuel that gives out heat and light energy when it burns. Coal is made from plants that died millions of years ago.

electricity A kind of energy. We use electricity to power machines and other things.

energy What gives people and machines the power they need to move and work.

fuel Something that burns and makes energy which we can use to work machines or power cars. Coal, gas, and oil are all kinds of fuel.

gas All around us, but we can't see it. We use gas for fuel.

gasoline Fuel made from oil. We put gasoline in our cars to give them the power they need to move.

gliding Flying without using power. Birds glide through the air without flapping their wings. The air helps birds to float for a short time.

hydroelectric power Electricity made using the energy of fast-flowing water. A hydroelectric power station makes electricity without burning fuel.

lightning Natural electricity made in clouds during a thunderstorm. Lightning appears as a flash of light in the sky.

machine Something we use that helps to make work easier.

oil A thick black liquid found underground. It is burned as a fuel, turned into gasoline and used to make materials such as plastic.

socket Where electricity comes into your home. You fit a plug into the socket to provide machines with electricity.

store To keep something to use later. You store food in a cupboard. A battery stores electricity. A piece of coal stores energy.

work What is done every time something moves, stops, gives out light or heat, or makes a noise. People and machines both work.

Index